CONTENTS

COOKERY NOTES

- Both metric and imperial measures are given for the recipes. Follow either metric or imperial throughout as they are not interchangeable.
- All spoon measures are level unless otherwise stated. Sets of measuring spoons are available in both metric and imperial for accurate measurements of small quantities.
- Ovens should be preheated to the specified temperature. Grills should also be preheated. The cooking times given in the recipes assume that this has been done.

- Where a stage is specified in brackets under freezing instructions, the dish should be frozen at the end of that stage.
- Size 2 eggs should be used except where otherwise specified. Free-range eggs are recommended.
- Use freshly ground black pepper and sea salt unless otherwise specified.
- Use fresh rather than dried herbs unless dried herbs are suggested in the recipe.
- Stocks should be freshly made if possible. Alternatively buy ready-made stocks or use good quality stock cubes.

INTRODUCTION

The shores of the warm Mediterranean sea border a large and varied area including the South of France, Spain, Italy, Greece, and – further afield – Turkey, the Middle East and North Africa.

For many of us the Mediterranean conjures up an image of sun-soaked summer holidays – pretty villages basking under brilliant blue skies, never far from the warm sea. One of travel's great pleasures is to sample local foods. The dishes are often familiar, accustomed as we are to international dishes. Cafés, bistros and pasta houses are commonplace everywhere today and cosmopolitan city dwellers can take their pick from different cuisines.

However, none of this familiarity detracts from the joy of the experience at first hand. There is the colourful chaos of a bustling food market in, say, Portugal or Greece where live poultry are sold alongside vegetables and herbs. In the Mediterranean fresh produce always looks larger than life. Vegetables, left to their own devices, have grown into amusing or grotesque shapes unlike the carefully cultivated specimens on our supermarket shelves. Fruits, ripened in the sun, have heady perfumes promising the sweetness of their flavours.

Street vendors are as likely to have a donkey as a van to peddle fruits by the kilo, or loaves of freshly baked bread – to households tucked away in narrow village backstreets. Shopping, or at least leisurely inquisitive shopping, is a real sensory indulgence.

Not only does the glorious climate produce sun-drenched fruits and flavoursome vegetables, there are the olive groves, nuts and grains which have such an influence on the Mediterranean diet. Many varieties of olives are produced, ranging from the tiny black ones from Nice to the plump green 'queen' olives of Spain. Greek kalamata olives have a particularly good flavour. Olive oil is, of course, used extensively in cooking and there are many varieties to choose from. Arguably the best source is Lucca in Tuscany, but good quality oil is produced in Spain, France and Greece too.

Throughout the Mediterranean you will also find interesting cheeses and other dairy produce made, most notably, from sheep's and goat's milk. Fragrant tender meat comes from animals which have lived and grazed on hills covered with aromatic wild thyme, fennel and rosemary. Of course, there is also a terrific wealth of seafood, fished fresh from the sea every day.

Added to all these culinary delights everyone appreciates how food always tastes better eaten outdoors in genial surroundings and in the company of warm-hearted and generous hosts. It brings a glow of pleasure and warmth just to recall experiences... such as sitting at a taverna table almost tottering into the water's edge enjoying that first Greek salad of the summer, with its salty feta cheese and cooling cucumber drizzled with olive oil. Or at other times, wrestling with the Spanish language to order tapas in a village bar, rather than give up and return to a more touristy establishment on the beaten track.

All across the Mediterranean there is a passion for food, and cooking and eating are considered to be among life's greatest pleasures. This book embraces the cooking of all the Mediterranean regions, inspired by many magical hours spent on sunny islands seeking out and devouring delicious food and drink.

Good Housekeeping
Cookery Club

MEDITERRANEAN

Lyn Rutherford

EBURY PRESS
LONDON

First published 1995

1 3 5 7 9 10 8 6 4 2

Text and Photography © Ebury Press 1995

First published in the United Kingdom in 1995 by Ebury Press,
Random House, 20 Vauxhall Bridge Road, London SW1V 2SA

Random House Australia (Pty) Limited
20 Alfred Street, Milsons Point, Sydney,
New South Wales 2061, Australia

Random House New Zealand Limited
18 Poland Road, Glenfield,
Auckland 10, New Zealand

Random House South Africa (Pty) Limited
PO Box 337, Bergvlei, South Africa

Random House UK Limited Reg. No. 954009

A CIP catalogue record for this book is available from the British Library.

Managing Editor: JANET ILLSLEY
Design: SARA KIDD
Special Photography: GRAHAM KIRK
Food Stylist: LYN RUTHERFORD
Photographic Stylist: HELEN PAYNE
Techniques Photography: KARL ADAMSON
Food Techniques Stylist: ANGELA KINGSBURY
Recipe Testing: EMMA-LEE GOW

ISBN 0 09 180702 6

Typeset in Gill Sans by Textype Typesetters, Cambridge
Colour Separations by Magnacraft, London
Printed and bound in Italy by New Interlitho Italia S.p.a., Milan

PREPARATION TECHNIQUES

A good fishmonger will happily clean and fillet your purchase of fresh fish for you, and most large supermarkets sell a good range of prepared seafood. However, if you prefer to prepare the fish yourself for the recipes in this book, the following step-by-step instructions make it easy to do so.

CLEANING MUSSELS

1. Rinse the mussels in plenty of fresh cold water to help rid them of any grittiness.

2. Scrub the mussel shells using a small, stiff brush to remove any grit and barnacles.

3. Pull off the hairy 'beard' which protrudes from the side of the shell.

4. At the same time, discard any mussels which do not close when squeezed, or tapped firmly with the back of a knife. Rinse the mussels again.

CLEANING CLAMS

Clams may not have beards but should be cleaned in the same way as mussels.

PREPARING SCALLOPS

I. Rinse the scallop shells well. Holding a scallop in your hand, rounded-side down, insert a sturdy knife in between the two shells.

2. Slide the blade across the flat shell to free the scallop. The shell should open. Discard the empty shell.

3. Carefully slide knife under the scallop to free it from the shell.

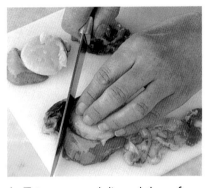

4. Trim away and discard the soft fringe-like part of the scallop and remove the tough 'connective' muscle and any dark parts.

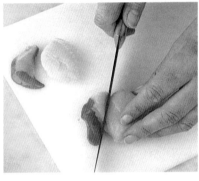

5. If required separate the roe or 'coral' from the white flesh of the scallop.

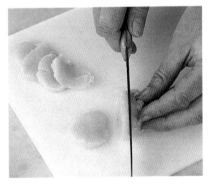

6. Halve or slice the scallop meat into rounds if necessary.

CLEANING SQUID

I. Pull the squid 'pouch' and the tentacles apart.

2. Cut the tentacles away from the head just below the eyes. Discard the head.

3. Using your fingers, remove the 'quill' and any soft innards from the pouch. Discard.

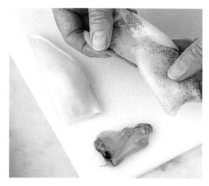

4. Peel off the thin layer of dark skin that covers the body and discard.

5. Rinse the tentacles and the squid pouch thoroughly under cold running water.

6. The cleaned squid pouch may now be sliced into rings.

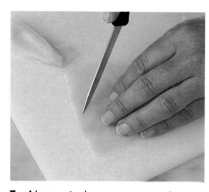

7. Alternatively, cut open to give large pieces and score using a small sharp knife.

CLEANING SARDINES AND REMOVING THEIR BACKBONES

1. Using a filleting knife, slit the sardines open along their bellies.

2. Scrape out any soft innards from the belly and behind the gills.

3. Rinse thoroughly under cold running water.

4. To remove the backbones, place the fish slit-side down on a board and, using your fingers, press firmly along the length of the backbone to loosen it from the flesh.

5. Turn the fish over and pull out the backbone through the slit in the belly. Use small scissors to cut the end of the backbone free inside the fish if necessary.

FILLETING RED MULLET

This technique also applies to mackerel and other 'round' fish.

1. Using a filleting knife, cut along the belly of the fish.

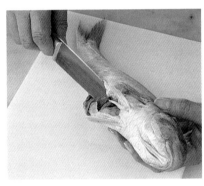

2. Scrape or pull out the innards.

3. Rinse thoroughly to remove all traces of blood.

4. Make a deep cut along the backbone from head to tail.

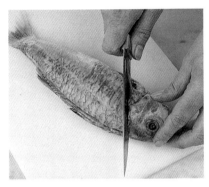

5. Cut through the skin and flesh just behind the gills to separate the fillet from the head.

6. Starting at the head, use the knife to loosen the flesh away from the bones, cutting with short strokes and keeping the knife in close contact with the bones.

7. Lift the fillet free with the other hand.

8. Turn the fish over and repeat the procedure on the other side, to remove the second fillet.

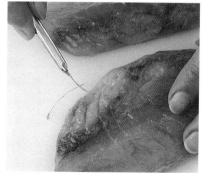

9. Pick out any bones left in the fillets using fingers or tweezers.

FISH SOUP WITH ROUILLE

Given the abundance of fish and seafood available in the Mediterranean it is not surprising that fish soups are popular all over the region. Most notable, perhaps, are the *bouillabaisse* of Provence and the *brodetto* of Italy, but similar recipes – using a mixture of fish and shellfish – are found elsewhere.

SERVES 6-8

900 g (2 lb) mixed white fish, eg red mullet, red snapper, cod, monkfish, whiting

450 g (1 lb) mackerel fillet

350 g (12 oz) mussels in shells

225 g (8 oz) raw prawns in shells (see note)

3 onions, peeled

handful of fresh parsley stalks

salt and pepper

2.5 ml (½ tsp) saffron strands

1 small fennel bulb, or 3 celery stalks

90 ml (6 tbsp) olive oil

3 garlic cloves, crushed

400 g (14 oz) can chopped tomatoes

1 strip of orange rind

1 bouquet garni

15 ml (1 tbsp) tomato purée

ROUILLE

2 garlic cloves

5 ml (1 tsp) cayenne pepper

2 egg yolks

90 ml (6 tbsp) olive oil

15 ml (1 tbsp) tomato purée

TO SERVE

45 ml (3 tbsp) roughly chopped parsley

toasted French bread

PREPARATION TIME
30 minutes
COOKING TIME 1½ hours
FREEZING Not suitable

650-485 CALS PER SERVING

1. Trim all the fish and cut into large chunks, reserving any heads, tails or other trimmings. Thoroughly clean the mussels (see page 6), discarding any which do not close when firmly tapped with a knife. Rinse the prawns.

2. Put all the fish trimmings in a large saucepan. Slice one of the onions and add to the pan with the parsley stalks, salt and pepper. Pour in 1.1 litre (2 pints) of water and bring to the boil. Lower the heat, cover and simmer for 30 minutes. Cool slightly, then strain the stock and set aside.

3. Crumble the saffron strands into a small bowl or cup, pour on about 45 ml (3 tbsp) boiling water and leave to stand.

4. Slice the remaining onions and chop the fennel or celery. Heat the olive oil in a large pan. Add the onions and fennel or celery; sauté for 5 minutes. Stir in the garlic, canned tomatoes with their juice, orange rind, bouquet garni, tomato purée, and saffron with its liquid. Season with salt and pepper. Bring to the boil and add the reserved fish stock. Bring back to the boil, then cover and simmer for 20 minutes.

5. Meanwhile, prepare the rouille. Peel and roughly chop the garlic. Put the garlic, cayenne and egg yolks in a food processor. Add a pinch of salt. Blend briefly to mix then, with the motor running, slowly trickle in the oil in a thin stream to give a thick consistency, as for mayonnaise. Add the tomato purée and adjust the seasoning to taste; the rouille should be quite spicy.

6. Bring the soup to a rapid boil and add the mackerel to the pan. Add the white fish, then scatter the mussels and prawns over the top. Boil for 6-8 minutes until the fish is opaque and flakes readily, and the mussel shells are open. Discard any mussels which do not open. Adjust the seasoning.

7. Serve the soup scattered with the freshly chopped parsley and accompanied by the rouille and toasted French bread.

NOTE: If raw prawns are unobtainable use cooked ones instead, but add them 2-3 minutes before the end of the cooking time to heat through.

TECHNIQUE

For the rouille, slowly trickle in the oil through the feeder tube while the motor is running.

CHICK PEA SOUP

Hearty and warming, this spiced soup with golden croûtons makes an excellent sustaining first course or it can be followed by a crisp salad for a complete light meal. A very popular pulse in the Mediterranean, chick peas are widely used in dips and salads, soups and stews. To save time you can prepare this soup using canned chick peas (see variation); they give quite a good result.

SERVES 6

225 g (8 oz) dried chick
   peas, soaked for at least 4
   hours, preferably overnight
1 onion
60 ml (4 tbsp) olive oil
2 garlic cloves, crushed
15 ml (1 tbsp) ground
   coriander
15 ml (1 tbsp) paprika
10 ml (2 tsp) ground cumin
2 fresh thyme sprigs
1.5 litres (2½ pints) chicken
   or vegetable stock
1 large potato, about 175 g
   (6 oz)
2 carrots
3 tomatoes
30 ml (2 tbsp) chopped fresh
   coriander
salt and pepper
15 ml (1 tbsp) tahini
   (sesame seed paste)
GARLIC CROÛTONS
50 g (2 oz) butter, softened
2 garlic cloves, crushed
4 thick slices white bread
TO GARNISH
coriander sprigs

PREPARATION TIME
20 minutes, plus soaking
COOKING TIME 1½ hours
FREEZING Suitable

390 CALS PER SERVING

1. Put the chick peas in a saucepan and add sufficient water to cover by 5 cm (2 inches). Bring to the boil, cover and boil rapidly for 15 minutes, then drain.

2. Meanwhile, peel and chop the onion. Heat the olive oil in a large saucepan, add the onion and sauté over a medium heat for 5 minutes, until softened. Add the garlic and spices and cook for a further 3 minutes.

3. Add the chick peas to the saucepan with the thyme and stock. Bring to the boil, then lower the heat, cover and cook for 40 minutes.

4. Meanwhile, peel and chop the potato; peel and slice the carrots. Immerse the tomatoes in a bowl of boiling water for 30 seconds, then drain and refresh under cold running water. Peel away the skins and roughly chop the flesh.

5. Add the potato, carrots and tomatoes to the pan. Stir in the chopped coriander and season with salt and pepper. Bring back to the boil, then lower the heat and simmer for a further 30-40 minutes until the chick peas and vegetables are tender. Stir in the tahini.

6. Using a food processor or blender, purée the soup, in batches if necessary, until fairly smooth. Taste and adjust the seasoning.

7. Shortly before serving, prepare the croûtons. Preheat the oven to 200°C (400°F) mark 6. In a small bowl, mix the butter and garlic together until evenly blended. Remove the crusts from the bread, then spread with the garlic butter. Cut into squares and place on a baking sheet. Bake for 8-10 minutes until crisp and golden. Sprinkle with salt.

8. Reheat the soup before serving in warmed bowls, garnished with coriander and accompanied by the hot croûtons.

VARIATION

Use two 400 g (14 oz) cans chick peas. Drain, rinse under cold running water and drain well. Add the stock and thyme to the soup with the vegetables and simmer for 30 minutes, then add the chick peas and cook for a further 10 minutes.

TECHNIQUE

Spread the slices of bread with the garlic butter, then cut into cubes.

GAZPACHO

This chilled tomato and pepper soup comes from Andalusia, in Spain. It has a refreshing flavour, pungent with garlic and sweet peppers. With its liberal garnishes of creamy hard-boiled egg, chopped vegetables, herbs and crisp croûtons, gazpacho is a joy to eat.

SERVES 6-8

700 g (1½ lb) flavourful ripe
   tomatoes
1 cucumber
1 red pepper
1 green pepper
1 red chilli
3 garlic cloves
225 g (8 oz) fresh
   wholemeal breadcrumbs
15 ml (1 tbsp) tomato purée
60 ml (4 tbsp) wine vinegar
90 ml (6 tbsp) olive oil
10 ml (2 tsp) salt
pepper
TO SERVE
chopped cucumber
red and green pepper slices
chopped hard-boiled egg
chopped red or mild onion
ice cubes
croûtons (see below)

PREPARATION TIME
25 minutes, plus chilling time
COOKING TIME
Nil
FREEZING
Suitable: Stage 4

310-230 CALS PER SERVING

1. First skin the tomatoes. Immerse in a bowl of boiling water, then drain and refresh under cold running water. Peel away the skins and roughly chop the flesh. Peel the cucumber and chop the flesh.

2. Halve, core and deseed the peppers, then chop roughly. Wearing rubber gloves to prevent skin irritation, halve the chilli, remove the seeds and roughly chop the flesh. Peel and chop the garlic.

3. Put the prepared vegetables and garlic into a large bowl. Add the breadcrumbs, tomato purée, wine vinegar, olive oil, salt and pepper to taste. Stir to mix together thoroughly.

4. Transfer half of the soup to a blender or food processor. Add about 300 ml (½ pint) water and process until fairly smooth. Transfer to a large serving bowl. Purée the remaining half of the soup mixture with another 300 ml (½ pint) water. Add to the puréed soup and stir well. Adjust the seasoning to taste. Cover with cling film and chill in the refrigerator for at least 2 hours.

5. To serve, put the garnishes in separate small bowls. Add a little ice to the gazpacho and serve accompanied by the garnishes.

CROÛTONS: To make these, cut 2.5 cm (1 inch) squares from 3-4 thick slices of day-old white bread. Fry in butter and oil, turning constantly, until crisp and golden. Drain on kitchen paper.

TECHNIQUE

Purée the soup in two batches, adding 300 ml (½ pint) water to each batch.

MEDITERRANEAN DIPS

Serve these dips simply, with some good bread and perhaps a little fruity olive oil. Alternatively accompany them with a colourful selection of fresh or grilled vegetables. All three dips are delicious spread on to hot crostini with roasted garlic purée.

SERVES 4-6

TAPENADE
45 ml (3 tbsp) capers
75 g (3 oz) stoned black olives
50 g (2 oz) can anchovy
   fillets, drained
100 ml (3½ fl oz) olive oil
30 ml (2 tbsp) brandy

WHITE BEAN DIP
1 onion
2 garlic cloves
60 ml (4 tbsp) olive oil
7.5 ml (1½ tsp) ground cumin
1.25 ml (¼ tsp) cayenne
   pepper
400 g (14 oz) can cannellini
   beans
juice of ½ lemon

HOT PEPPER DIP
1 large red pepper
2 red chillies
2 garlic cloves, crushed
2 egg yolks
200 ml (7 fl oz) light olive oil

TO SERVE
fresh and/or grilled vegetables,
   such as asparagus, peppers,
   tomatoes, etc
toasted French bread
roasted garlic (optional)

PREPARATION TIME
30 minutes
COOKING TIME
20 minutes
FREEZING Suitable

1. To make the tapenade, rinse the capers and put in a blender or food processor with the olives and anchovies. Process briefly to chop. While the motor is running, add the olive oil in a steady stream. Stir in the brandy and season with pepper to taste. Transfer to a serving bowl.

2. To prepare the white bean dip, peel and chop the onion and garlic. Heat the oil in a frying pan, add the onion and cook, stirring, over a medium heat for 5 minutes until softened. Add the garlic and spices and cook for a further 3 minutes.

3. Meanwhile, drain and rinse the cannellini beans. Transfer the onion mixture to a blender or food processor, add the beans and lemon juice and purée until fairly smooth. Season with salt and pepper to taste. Transfer to a serving bowl.

4. For the hot pepper dip, preheat the grill to high. Halve the red pepper lengthwise and place skin-side up on the grill rack with the whole chillies. Grill for about 10 minutes until the skins are charred and blistered all over; turn the chillies halfway through cooking. Allow to cool slightly, then remove the skins. Slit the chillies open and rinse out the seeds under cold running water.

5. Roughly chop the red pepper and chilli flesh and put in a blender or food

processor. Add the garlic and egg yolks. With the motor running, add the oil in a slow trickle. Season with salt and pepper to taste. Spoon into a serving bowl.

6. Serve the dips accompanied by a platter of fresh and/or grilled vegetables, toasted French bread and roasted garlic if desired.

CALORIE COUNTS: For each dip, the calorie content is as follows: Tapenade 295–195 cals per serving; White Bean Dip 245–165 cals per serving; Hot Pepper Dip 495–300 cals per serving.

TECHNIQUE

For the tapenade, put the capers, olives and anchovies in a food processor and process briefly to chop.

ONION TARTLETS WITH TOMATO AND CAPER SAUCE

Sweet caramelised onions, fresh basil and toasted pine nuts make a delicious filling for these simple-to-prepare puff pastry tartlets. They are complemented by a piquant sauce of fresh and sun-dried tomatoes flavoured with chilli and capers.

SERVES 4

450 g (1 lb) onions
30 ml (2 tbsp) olive or
 sunflower oil
about 300 g (10 oz) puff
 pastry, fresh or frozen and
 thawed
25 g (1 oz) pine nuts, toasted
12 basil leaves, shredded
salt and pepper
a little milk, to glaze
SAUCE
1 tomato
1 red chilli
25 g (1 oz) sun-dried
 tomatoes in oil, drained
25 g (1 oz) capers
15 ml (1 tbsp) olive oil

PREPARATION TIME
25 minutes
COOKING TIME
35 minutes
FREEZING
Not suitable

490 CALS PER SERVING

1. Preheat the oven to 220°C (425°F) Mark 7.

2. Peel and slice the onions. Heat the oil in a large frying pan, add the onions and cook over a low heat, stirring occasionally, for about 20 minutes until golden brown and caramelised.

3. Meanwhile, roll out the puff pastry on a lightly floured surface to a 3-5 mm (⅛-¼ inch) thickness. Using a saucepan lid or small plate as a guide, cut four 15 cm (6 inch) circles. Knock up the edges using a round-bladed knife and flute them decoratively. Place the pastry discs on a greased baking sheet and prick with a fork.

4. Add the pine nuts and basil to the caramelised onions and season with salt and pepper to taste. Divide the mixture between the pastry discs, leaving a 2.5 cm (½ inch) clear margin around the edges. Brush the edges with a little milk to glaze, then bake in the oven for about 15 minutes until well risen, crisp and golden brown.

5. While the tarts are baking, prepare the sauce. Halve, deseed and finely chop the tomato and place in a small bowl. Halve and deseed the chilli. Chop the sun-dried tomatoes, capers and chilli together on a board and add to the bowl with the olive oil. Mix well, seasoning with salt and pepper to taste.

6. Serve the tartlets hot or warm, accompanied by the sauce.

TECHNIQUE

Knock up the edges of the pastry discs, using a round-bladed knife.

FILO PIES

Little triangular pies made from paper-thin filo pastry can be stuffed with a variety of tasty fillings and served as part of a Greek *meze* or first course, or as a snack. These mouth-watering filo triangles are at their best served warm, fresh from the oven.

MAKES ABOUT 44

450 g (1 lb) frozen filo pastry, thawed
olive oil, for brushing
FETA AND HERB FILLING
300 g (10 oz) feta cheese
60 ml (4 tbsp) pine nuts
30 ml (2 tbsp) chopped fresh parsley or coriander
15 ml (1 tbsp) chopped fresh dill
½ egg, lightly beaten
pinch of freshly grated nutmeg
pepper
OLIVE, EGG AND ANCHOVY FILLING
3 hard-boiled eggs
50 g (2 oz) pitted olives
3 anchovy fillets
30 ml (2 tbsp) roughly chopped walnuts
30 ml (2 tbsp) chopped fresh parsley or chervil
pepper

PREPARATION TIME
30 minutes
COOKING TIME
20-25 minutes
FREEZING
Not suitable

100-75 CALS PER PIE

1. First prepare the fillings. For the feta and herb filling, preheat the grill to medium. Crumble the cheese into a bowl. Toast the pine nuts on a baking sheet under the grill, turning occasionally, until golden. Let cool slightly, then add to the cheese with the herbs, egg, nutmeg and pepper to taste. Mix well.

2. For the olive, egg and anchovy filling, chop the hard-boiled eggs and put into a small bowl. Finely chop the olives and anchovy fillets together and add to the bowl with the walnuts, parsley or chervil. Mix well and season with pepper to taste.

3. Preheat the oven to 190°C (375°F) Mark 5. Grease two baking sheets.

4. Cut the filo pastry sheets into strips, each about 10 x 25 cm (4 x 10 inches). Keep them covered with a damp cloth while not in use to prevent them drying out.

5. Working with 3 or 4 strips at a time, brush with oil and place a heaped 5 ml spoonful (teaspoon) of one of the fillings at the top right-hand corner of each strip. Fold the corner down to make a triangle and continue to flip the filled triangle down the length of the filo strip to wrap in the pastry. Place the filo triangles on a baking sheet and brush with a little more oil. Repeat to use up all of the filo strips and both fillings.

6. Bake the filo pies in the oven for 20-25 minutes until crisp and deep golden in colour. Serve hot or warm.

VARIATION

For the olive filling, replace the anchovy fillets with 3 sun-dried tomatoes. Use basil instead of parsley if you prefer.

TECHNIQUE

Place a heaped teaspoonful of filling at the top right-hand corner of the filling, then fold the corner down to make a triangle.

STUFFED SARDINES WITH CAPERS AND HERBS

Bursting with flavour and redolent of much of the Mediterranean region, sardines are always best cooked simply. They need only a hint of acidity to counteract their oily nature – a squeeze of lemon will do! Here, with a stuffing enlivened with capers and herbs, the simple sardine becomes a gourmet treat. Serve as a starter, or with a crisp salad and/or new potatoes as a light meal.

SERVES 4

8 large fresh sardines
15 ml (1 tbsp) lemon juice
15 ml (1 tbsp) olive oil
STUFFING
50 g (2 oz) fresh white
   breadcrumbs
2 garlic cloves, crushed
45 ml (3 tbsp) chopped fresh
   parsley
30 ml (2 tbsp) capers,
   chopped
5 ml (1 tsp) grated lemon
   rind
60 ml (4 tbsp) olive oil
salt and pepper

PREPARATION TIME
30 minutes
COOKING TIME
20 minutes
FREEZING
Not suitable

460 CALS PER SERVING

1. Preheat the oven to 180°C (350°F) Mark 4.

2. Slit the sardines open along their bellies and clean thoroughly (see page 8). Carefully loosen the backbones by pressing along them firmly (see technique). Turn the fish over and pull out the bone through the opening in the belly. Leave the heads and tails intact.

3. For the stuffing, mix together the breadcrumbs, garlic, parsley, capers, lemon rind and oil. Season with salt and pepper to taste.

4. Using a teaspoon, spoon the stuffing into the fish cavities, dividing it equally between them.

5. Arrange the sardines, head to tail, in a large oiled ovenproof dish in which they fit snugly. Drizzle over the lemon juice and olive oil. Bake in the oven for about 20 minutes until cooked through. Serve immediately.

VARIATION

Grilled Sardines: Omit the stuffing. Clean the sardines, removing their backbones, then arrange on a grill rack. Mix together 75 ml (5 tbsp) olive oil, 30 ml (2 tbsp) lemon juice, 5 ml (1 tsp) grated lemon rind, 45 ml (3 tbsp) chopped fresh parsley and seasoning to taste. Drizzle this mixture over the sardines and grill for 5-7 minutes each side, basting frequently. Serve hot or cold.

TECHNIQUE

To loosen the backbone, place the fish slit-side down on a board and press firmly along the length of the bone.

GRILLED STUFFED MUSSELS

These appetising morsels are easy to eat and tend to disappear quickly, served as they are, hot from the grill. It's a good idea to eke them out further with a crisp salad and freshly baked bread.

SERVES 4-6

1.4 kg (3 lb) large mussels in
   their shells
75 ml (5 tbsp) dry white
   wine
2 slices Parma ham or other
   prosciutto
25 g (1 oz) fresh white
   breadcrumbs
45 ml (3 tbsp) chopped fresh
   parsley
15 ml (1 tbsp) chopped fresh
   oregano
1-2 garlic cloves, crushed
salt and pepper
75 ml (5 tbsp) olive oil
lemon wedges, to serve

PREPARATION TIME
15 minutes
COOKING TIME
5-6 minutes
FREEZING
Not suitable

325-215 CALS PER SERVING

1. Clean the mussels thoroughly and remove their 'beards' (see page 6). Rinse well and discard any that do not close when tapped firmly.

2. Put the mussels in a large saucepan with the white wine. Cover with a tight-fitting lid and bring to the boil. Cook over a high heat for 3-4 minutes or until the mussel shells open. Strain, reserving the liquid. Discard any mussels that have not opened.

3. Remove and discard the empty half-shell from each mussel. Arrange the mussels in their half-shells on baking sheets.

4. Finely chop the Parma ham or prosciutto and place in a bowl with the breadcrumbs, herbs and garlic. Season with salt and pepper to taste. Add half of the olive oil and moisten with a little of the reserved mussel liquor, mixing with a fork.

5. Preheat the grill to high. Spoon the breadcrumb mixture over the mussels on their shells, dividing it equally between them. Sprinkle with the remaining olive oil and place under the grill for about 2 minutes until the crumb mixture is crisp and golden. Serve hot, accompanied by lemon wedges.

VARIATION

For a more economical version, replace the Parma ham with 2 rashers smoked bacon. Finely dice the bacon and dry-fry in its own fat until beginning to crisp, then mix with the other stuffing ingredients. Stuff the mussels as above and sprinkle with freshly grated Parmesan before grilling.

TECHNIQUE

Spoon the breadcrumb mixture over the mussels, covering them well.

SPAGHETTI ALLE VONGOLE

If you cannot obtain fresh clams for this classic pasta sauce, try making it with mussels instead. Pasta, simple as it is, must be properly cooked to taste good. The secret of success here lies in the final stage where the pasta finishes cooking in the juicy sauce.

SERVES 4

1 kg (2 lb) fresh clams

450 g (1 lb) plum tomatoes

salt and pepper

3 garlic cloves

75 ml (5 tbsp) extra-virgin olive oil

100 ml (3½ fl oz) dry white wine

15 ml (1 tbsp) chopped fresh oregano

400 g (14 oz) dried spaghetti

30 ml (2 tbsp) chopped fresh parsley

40 g (1½ oz) butter

PREPARATION TIME
20 minutes
COOKING TIME
About 10 minutes
FREEZING
Not suitable

690 CALS PER SERVING

1. Wash the clams in plenty of cold water and scrub the shells with a small brush. Leave to soak in a bowl of fresh cold water for 10 minutes, then rinse again and drain well. Discard any shells which do not close if they are tapped firmly with the back of a knife.

2. Immerse the tomatoes in a bowl of boiling water for 30 seconds, then drain and refresh under cold running water. Peel away the skins and roughly chop the flesh. Bring a large pan of salted water to the boil, for the pasta.

3. Peel and slice the garlic. Heat the olive oil in a large frying pan (one which will be large enough to hold and toss the spaghetti later). Add the garlic and cook over a medium heat for 2 minutes; do not let it brown. Stir in the tomatoes and the white wine.

4. Add the cleaned clams in their shells to the pan. Season with salt and pepper, stir well and bring to the boil. Cover with a tight-fitting lid and cook for 2-3 minutes to steam open the clams. Stir in the oregano and remove from the heat.

5. Meanwhile, add the spaghetti to the pan of boiling water. Cook for about 5 minutes; the pasta should be firm and not yet quite *al dente*. Drain well.

6. Just before serving, return the clam sauce to heat and stir in the chopped parsley. Add the drained spaghetti to the pan and cook for 1 minute. The pasta should finish its cooking in the juices of the clams. Add the butter, toss lightly and serve at once.

VARIATION

If clams are unobtainable, use fresh mussels instead. Prepare as for clams.

TECHNIQUE

Tap any clams with open shells firmly with the back of a knife. Discard any which do not close as they are unlikely to be fresh enough to eat.

SEARED SQUID WITH ROASTED PLUM TOMATOES AND HERB SALAD

Plum tomatoes are roasted to intensify their sweet flavour in this glorious salad. With lots of fresh herbs and tasty salad leaves, such as rocket and chicory, they are a perfect foil for succulent seared squid.

SERVES 4

575 g (1¼ lb) squid
90 ml (6 tbsp) extra-virgin
   olive oil
2 garlic cloves
coarse sea salt and pepper
30 ml (2 tbsp) chopped fresh
   basil
8 small plum tomatoes
3 fresh rosemary sprigs
about 75 g (3 oz) mixed
   salad leaves, such as
   rocket, lamb's lettuce
   (mâche), frisée, chicory
juice of 1 small lemon
handful of freshly torn flat-
   leaf parsley

PREPARATION TIME
20 minutes
COOKING TIME
50-55 minutes
FREEZING
Not suitable

340 CALS PER SERVING

1. Preheat the oven to 200°C (400°F) Mark 6.

2. Clean the squid (following the step-by-step instructions on pages 7-8). Cut the body pouches into even-sized pieces, about 7.5 cm (3 inches) square, and score a lattice pattern on each piece. Leave the tentacles whole.

3. Place the squid in a bowl and spoon over 45 ml (3 tbsp) of the olive oil. Peel the garlic cloves and crush them to a paste on a chopping board with a little coarse sea salt. Add to the squid with the chopped basil. Season with pepper and mix well. Cover and leave in the refrigerator while preparing the tomatoes.

4. Cut the tomatoes in half lengthwise. Place them, cut-side up, in one layer, in a shallow baking tin. Tuck the rosemary sprigs among them and season liberally with coarse sea salt. Drizzle over the remaining olive oil. Roast in the oven for 40-45 minutes until tender but still holding their shape.

5. To cook the squid, preheat a dry (not oiled) cast-iron griddle over a high heat for 5 minutes. Lower the heat to medium.

6. Add the squid to the hot griddle pan in one layer; you may need to cook them in two batches. Allow to sizzle undis-turbed for 1 minute, then turn each piece and cook the other side for 1 minute. Add to the roasted tomatoes. Discard the rosemary sprigs.

7. Put the salad leaves in a serving bowl and top with the squid and tomatoes. Add the lemon juice to the pan and heat, scraping up the flavoursome bits from the bottom as it sizzles. Trickle over the squid and tomatoes and sprinkle with the parsley. Toss lightly and serve at once.

TECHNIQUE

Using a sharp knife, score the squid flesh to create a lattice pattern on each piece.

GRILLED VEGETABLE AND SEAFOOD PLATTER

An abundance of seafood and grilled vegetables makes a colourful Mediterranean feast. Served with garlicky mayonnaise, this platter is equally good hot or cold, as a main course or lavish starter.

SERVES 4-6

350 g (12 oz) baby red
   potatoes
salt and pepper
300 ml (½ pint) light olive oil
grated rind of 1 lemon
20 ml (4 tsp) chopped oregano
30 ml (2 tbsp) chopped dill
225 g (8 oz) baby squid
225 g (8 oz) raw tiger prawns
225 g (8 oz) shelled scallops,
   cleaned (see page 7)
3 small onions
2 courgettes
2 small red peppers
2 small yellow peppers
2 fresh rosemary sprigs
15-30 ml (1-2 tbsp) balsamic
   vinegar
AIOLI
2 egg yolks
15 ml (1 tbsp) wine vinegar
5 ml (1 tsp) Dijon mustard
300 ml (½ pint) olive oil
3 garlic cloves, crushed
TO GARNISH
oregano sprigs

PREPARATION TIME
25 minutes, plus marinating
COOKING TIME
25-30 minutes
FREEZING Not suitable

820-545 CALS PER SERVING

1. Parboil the baby red potatoes in boiling salted water for 10-12 minutes until almost tender. Drain and return to the pan to dry.

2. In a small bowl mix together the olive oil, lemon rind, oregano and dill for the marinade.

3. Clean the squid (see pages 7-8) and cut each body pouch in half. Using a small sharp knife, score a lattice pattern on each piece. Rinse the prawns, drain and pat dry. Place all the seafood in a shallow dish and spoon over half of the marinade. Mix well and leave to marinate for at least 1 hour.

4. Meanwhile make the aioli. Put the egg yolks in a bowl with the vinegar, mustard and salt and pepper to taste. Slowly add the olive oil in a steady stream, whisking constantly until all the oil is added and the mayonnaise is smooth and thick. Stir in the crushed garlic and leave to stand, while preparing the vegetables.

5. Peel and quarter the onions. Cut the courgettes into 1 cm (½ inch) thick slices. Cut the red and yellow peppers into quarters discarding the cores and seeds. Put all the vegetables, including the par-boiled potatoes, in a bowl. Add the remaining marinade and the rosemary sprigs. Toss to coat thoroughly.

6. Preheat the grill to high. Line the grill pan and a baking sheet with foil. Tip the vegetables and marinade into the grill pan. Grill for about 20 minutes, turning frequently, until the vegetables are tender and lightly patched with brown. Set the grill pan lower (to keep the vegetables hot).

7. Tip the seafood and their marinade onto the prepared baking sheet. Grill for 6-8 minutes, until cooked through, turning frequently and basting with the marinade.

8. Arrange the vegetables and seafood on a large platter or individual plates and drizzle with a little balsamic vinegar. Garnish with oregano sprigs and serve accompanied by the aioli.

NOTE: The calorie count assumes that half the aioli will be eaten with the fish.

TECHNIQUE

Spoon half the marinade over the seafood and toss well.

GRILLED FISH STEAKS WITH LEMON AND CAPER SAUCE

With its flavoursome marinade and piquant sauce, this recipe is most suited to the firm-textured, 'meaty' fish steaks of the Mediterranean – such as tuna, swordfish and grouper. However, you could also try it with other fish steaks, such as cod or salmon, if you prefer.

SERVES 4

4 tuna or swordfish steaks, each about 200 g (7 oz)
2 garlic cloves
5 ml (1 tsp) chopped fresh thyme
5 ml (1 tsp) chopped fresh oregano
salt and pepper
200 ml (7 fl oz) dry white wine
15 ml (1 tbsp) olive oil
SAUCE
5 ml (1 tsp) finely grated lemon rind
30 ml (2 tbsp) capers in wine vinegar, drained and rinsed
juice of 2 small lemons
75 ml (5 tbsp) olive oil

PREPARATION TIME
10 minutes, plus marinating
COOKING TIME
About 15 minutes
FREEZING
Not suitable

505 CALS PER SERVING

1. Arrange the fish in one layer in a shallow dish. Peel and finely chop the garlic. Sprinkle the garlic and chopped herbs over the fish, and season with salt and pepper. Pour on the white wine and leave to marinate for 1-2 hours, turning occasionally.

2. Preheat the grill to medium. Lift the fish steaks out onto the grill rack, reserving the marinade. Brush the fish with olive oil. Grill for about 7 minutes each side, until firm and cooked through, basting frequently with the reserved marinade.

3. Meanwhile, make the sauce. Put the lemon rind, capers and lemon juice in a blender and process briefly. With the machine running, pour in the olive oil and blend together. Season with salt and pepper to taste.

4. To serve, arrange the fish on warmed serving plates and spoon the sauce around. Serve with new potatoes and a crisp salad or vegetables.

VARIATION

Use salmon or cod steaks instead of the tuna or swordfish steaks.

TECHNIQUE

Baste the fish steaks frequently with the marinade during grilling, to prevent them becoming dry.

BASED SEA BASS WITH ANCHOVIES AND HERBS

This magnificent whole baked fish – accompanied with vegetables or a salad, good bread and chilled white wine – makes a splendid meal worthy of a special occasion. Sea bass with its fine delicate flesh is the supreme choice, but you could use a less expensive fish, such as grey mullet, red pepper or salmon trout.

SERVES 4

1 sea bass, about 1.2 kg
 (2½ lb), cleaned
pepper
2 garlic cloves, peeled and
 chopped
4 fresh rosemary sprigs
1 sprig of fresh bay leaves
5 fresh basil sprigs
45 ml (3 tbsp) olive oil
6 canned anchovy fillets,
 drained
50 g (2 oz) stale white
 breadcrumbs (one-day
 old)
TO SERVE
extra herb sprigs, to garnish
lemon wedges, to serve

PREPARATION TIME
5 minutes
COOKING TIME
40 minutes
FREEZING
Not suitable

425 CALS PER SERVING

1. Preheat the oven to 180°C (350°F) Mark 4.

2. Lightly oil a baking dish or tin large enough to hold the fish. Rinse the fish inside and out, then pat dry. Season the cavity with pepper and spread with the garlic. Lay the rosemary and bay leaves in the bottom of the baking tin and place the fish on top. Put the basil leaves into the fish cavity.

3. Heat the oil in a small pan. Add the anchovies and cook gently for 1-2 minutes until dissolved, stirring with a fork to help break them up.

4. Spoon the crushed anchovies over the fish. Sprinkle the breadcrumbs on top and bake in the oven for 40 minutes, until the fish is cooked through and the flesh flakes easily.

5. Carefully lift the fish onto a warmed serving platter and surround with extra herb sprigs to garnish. Serve at once, accompanied by lemon wedges and seasonal vegetables or a salad.

VARIATION

Instead of sea bass, use grey mullet, sea bream, red snapper or salmon trout.

TECHNIQUE

Insert the basil leaves into the cavity of the fish to impart flavour during baking.

BAKED RED MULLET WITH ROSEMARY AND LEMON

Rosy-skinned and white-fleshed, the handsome red mullet is a favourite Mediterranean fish. In Greece it is typically seasoned with rosemary, lemon and a drizzle of olive oil, then baked in a hot oven to crisp perfection and served with skordalia – a pungent garlicky sauce. Make the sauce first to allow time for the flavours to develop.

SERVES 4

8 small or 4 large red mullet

8 fresh rosemary sprigs, halved

1 lemon, thinly sliced

120 ml (8 tbsp) dry white wine

60 ml (4 tbsp) olive oil

salt and pepper

SKORDALIA

3 garlic cloves

40 g (1½ oz) crustless white bread

125 g (4 oz) ground almonds

coarse sea salt

100 ml (3½ fl oz) light olive oil, or olive oil and sunflower oil mixed

juice of ½ lemon

TO GARNISH

lemon wedges

PREPARATION TIME
15 minutes
COOKING TIME
20 minutes
FREEZING
Not suitable

680 CALS PER SERVING

1. First make the skordalia. Crush the garlic cloves and place in a blender or food processor. Moisten the bread with a little cold water and squeeze out the excess by hand to give a sticky paste. Add to the food processor with the ground almonds and a little sea salt. Process briefly, then with the motor running, slowly drizzle in the oil, as for making mayonnaise, to give a smooth sauce. Add the lemon juice and check the seasoning. Set aside.

2. Preheat the oven to 220°C (425°F) Mark 7. With a sharp knife make slashes in the sides of each fish. Tuck a rosemary sprig and a slice of lemon into the cavity of each fish and season with salt and pepper.

3. Arrange the fish, head to tail, in a large baking dish or roasting tin. Tuck the rest of the lemon slices in between the fish. Scatter over the remaining rosemary sprigs. Drizzle over the white wine and olive oil. Bake for about 20 minutes until the fish flakes easily, basting halfway through cooking.

4. Serve the red mullet with the garlic sauce, accompanied by a crisp salad and some good bread.

VARIATION

Flavour the fish with oregano or thyme sprigs instead of rosemary.

TECHNIQUE

Using a sharp knife, make three diagonal slashes in the side of each fish.

PAELLA

The national dish of Spain, paella is traditionally cooked in a large open shallow pan, called a *paellera*. Rice and saffron are the only essential ingredients as paella can be vegetarian, or based simply on fish or meat, or – as here – a veritable feast with seafood, chicken and chorizo.

SERVES 6

4 boneless chicken thighs, skinned

350 g (12 oz) squid

450 g (1 lb) fresh mussels in their shells

225 g (8 oz) monkfish fillet

6 raw king prawns or langoustines

150 ml (¼ pint) dry white wine or water

10 ml (2 tsp) chopped fresh thyme

salt and pepper

1.2 litres (2 pints) chicken stock

1 large onion

225 g (8 oz) chorizo sausage

1 red pepper

3 large ripe tomatoes

60 ml (4 tbsp) olive oil

generous pinch of saffron threads

10 ml (2 tsp) paprika

3 garlic cloves, crushed

350 g (12 oz) long-grain rice

125 g (4 oz) frozen peas, thawed

TO SERVE

lemon wedges

PREPARATION TIME
10-15 minutes
COOKING TIME 40 minutes
FREEZING Not suitable

700 CALS PER SERVING

1. First prepare the chicken and seafood. Cut each chicken thigh into 3 pieces. Clean the squid and slice into rings (see pages 7-8). Clean the mussels and remove their 'beards' (see page 6); discard any that do not open when tapped firmly. Cut the monkfish into 2.5 cm (1 inch) pieces. Rinse the prawns or langoustines and keep whole.

2. Put the wine or water and chopped thyme into a large saucepan and add a little pepper. Bring to the boil and add the mussels. Cover with a tight-fitting lid and steam for a few minutes until the shells open. Drain, reserving the liquor; discard any unopened mussels.

3. Remove about half of the mussels from their shells. Set all the mussels aside. Add the reserved cooking liquor to the chicken stock.

4. Peel and chop the onion. Slice the chorizo; halve, core and deseed the red pepper, then chop the flesh. Immerse the tomatoes in a bowl of boiling water for 30 seconds, then drain and refresh under cold running water. Peel away the skins and chop the flesh.

5. Heat the olive oil in a paella pan or large deep frying pan over a medium high heat. Add the chicken pieces and cook, turning, for a few minutes until browned. Using a slotted spoon, transfer the chicken to a plate and set aside. Add the onion to the pan and cook for 5 minutes or until softened. Add the chorizo and red pepper and cook for 3 minutes.

6. Add the saffron, tomatoes, paprika and garlic to the pan. Cook for 1 minute, then stir in the rice and a little salt. Cook for a few minutes until the rice begins to look transparent. Meanwhile, heat the stock.

7. Add about half of the stock to the rice mixture. Bring to simmering point and cook for 5 minutes. Pour on the remaining stock and place the chicken pieces, monkfish, squid and prawns or langoustines on top. Simmer gently for about 15 minutes until the rice is tender; at this stage avoid stirring up the rice if possible. Towards the end of the cooking time stir in the peas and mussels. Adjust the seasoning to taste and serve at once, with lemon wedges.

TECHNIQUE

Drain the mussels, using a fine sieve, reserving the cooking liquor.

CHICKEN OR RABBIT WITH OLIVES AND FENNEL

Y ou can make this dish with either chicken or rabbit. If using chicken, buy leg and thigh portions as these will be more succulent than white breast meat. Serve with buttered pasta ribbons or rice and a simply cooked vegetable, such as steamed French beans or runner beans.

SERVES 4

8 small chicken or rabbit pieces, skinned
salt and pepper
1 fresh thyme sprig
1 fresh rosemary sprig
2 fresh bay leaves
1 large onion
4 garlic cloves
60 ml (4 tbsp) olive oil
10 ml (2 tsp) fennel seeds, crushed
200 ml (7 fl oz) dry white wine
12 black olives
12 stoned green olives, sliced
torn parsley or fennel leaves, to garnish

PREPARATION TIME
10 minutes
COOKING TIME
About 45 minutes
FREEZING
Suitable: Stage 3

455 CALS PER SERVING

1. Season the chicken or rabbit pieces with salt and pepper. Tie all the herbs together in a bundle, using cotton string. Peel and slice the onion; peel and halve the garlic cloves.

2. Heat the oil in a large, heavy sauté pan over a fairly high heat. Add the chicken or rabbit portions and brown them quickly on all sides. Lower the heat to medium.

3. Add the herbs, onion, garlic and fennel seeds to the pan and cook, stirring frequently, for about 5 minutes until the onion is softened. Stir in the wine. Bring to the boil, then lower the heat, cover and cook for 25-30 minutes until the poultry is cooked through. Remove the herbs.

4. Using a slotted spoon, transfer the chicken or rabbit pieces to a warmed serving platter and keep hot. Stir the juices in the pan thoroughly with a wooden spoon to break up the garlic. Add the whole and sliced olives to the pan and cook, uncovered, for about 5 minutes to reduce the sauce by about one third. Check the seasoning.

5. Pour the sauce over the chicken or rabbit and serve sprinkled with roughly torn fennel or parsley leaves.

NOTE: As the olives are quite salty, you may not need to add salt to this recipe.

TECHNIQUE

Tie the herbs together with cotton string to make a bouquet garni.

CHICKEN AND CHORIZO CASSEROLE

For this Spanish dish, buy the spiciest chorizo sausage you can find – to impart a rich flavour and colour. Serve with rice or potatoes, a crisp salad and a glass of red wine.

SERVES 4

8 small chicken joints, or
  1 chicken, about 1.6 kg
  (3½ lb), jointed
salt and pepper
1 onion
4 large or 8 small shallots
2 garlic cloves
225 g (8 oz) chorizo
  sausage, sliced
45 ml (3 tbsp) olive oil
two 400 g (14 oz) cans plum
  tomatoes
150 ml (¼ pint) dry white
  wine
30 ml (2 tbsp) chopped fresh
  parsley
2 fresh rosemary sprigs
1 strip of orange peel
2 red peppers, or 1 red and
  1 yellow pepper
TO GARNISH
handful of torn parsley
  leaves
handful of black olives
  (optional)

PREPARATION TIME
20 minutes
COOKING TIME
About 1 hour
FREEZING
Suitable: Stage 5

670 CALS PER SERVING

1. Season the chicken joints with salt and pepper. Peel and chop the onion. Peel the shallots. Peel and slice the garlic. Slice the chorizo sausage.

2. Heat the oil in a large heavy-based sauté pan (which has a lid). Add the chicken pieces and brown on all sides over a fairly high heat. Transfer to a plate, cover and set aside.

3. Add the onion and whole shallots to the sauté pan and cook over a medium heat, stirring frequently, for about 10 minutes until the onion is soft and golden and the shallots are lightly browned. Stir in the garlic and chorizo and continue cooking for 3-4 minutes until the juices begin to run from the chorizo.

4. Meanwhile, drain the tomatoes, reserving the juice, and roughly chop them. Add the wine and herbs to the pan together with the orange peel and tomatoes with their juice. Return the chicken to the pan. Bring to the boil, lower the heat, cover and simmer for 40-45 minutes until the chicken is tender.

5. Meanwhile, preheat the grill to high. Halve and deseed the peppers, then place, skin-side up, on the grill rack. Grill for about 10 minutes until the skins are blistered and blackened all over. Place in

a covered bowl and allow to cool slightly, then peel away the skins. Cut the flesh into thin strips. Add to the pan about 5 minutes before the chicken will be ready.

6. Lift out the chicken pieces using a slotted spoon and set aside. Increase the heat and boil steadily for a few minutes to reduce and thicken the sauce, then return the chicken to the pan. Adjust the seasoning. Serve hot, sprinkled with torn parsley leaves and a handful of black olives, if liked.

TECHNIQUE

Brown the chicken pieces over a fairly high heat, turning to ensure they are evenly coloured.

KLEFTIKO

Kleftiko – or 'Robber's Lamb' as it is literally translated – is a traditional Greek dish in which the lamb is seasoned simply with lemon and oregano and then cooked in a covered dish until meltingly tender. Serve with new potatoes and a green vegetable or salad.

SERVES 4

8 lamb loin chops, or 4 leg
    steaks (with bone)
2 lemons
15 ml (1 tbsp) dried oregano
salt and pepper
30 ml (2 tbsp) olive oil
2 onions
2 bay leaves
150 ml (¼ pint) dry white
    wine
150 ml (¼ pint) stock
TO GARNISH
lemon wedges
torn flat-leaf parsley
    (optional)

PREPARATION TIME
15 minutes, plus marinating
COOKING TIME
2-2½ hours
FREEZING
Suitable

350 CALS PER SERVING

1. Place the lamb in a single layer in a shallow dish. Squeeze the juice from the lemons into a small bowl or cup and add the oregano, salt and pepper. Sprinkle the mixture over the meat and leave to marinate in a cool place for at least 4 hours, preferably overnight.

2. Preheat the oven to 160°C (325°F) Mark 3. Heat the oil in a large frying pan. Lift the lamb chops out of the marinade and add them to the pan. Cook over a high heat, turning until well browned on all sides, then transfer to a shallow earthenware casserole.

3. Peel and slice the onions and add to the lamb, together with the bay leaves, wine and stock. Pour in any remaining marinade and season with pepper.

4. Cover the dish with foil. Bake in the oven for 2-2½ hours until the lamb is tender, removing the foil for the last 20 minutes to brown the meat.

5. Before serving, carefully skim off any excess fat. Serve the meat with the juices spooned over. Garnish with lemon wedges and torn parsley if desired.

NOTE: To extract the maximum amount of juice from the lemons, briefly warm them in a microwave oven before squeezing.

TECHNIQUE

Sprinkle the lemon and oregano mixture over the meat and leave to marinate for at least 4 hours.

TORTELLONI

Shaping these delightful tortelloni by hand is not a difficult task but it does require patience! A pasta machine will make rolling out the dough much easier. Serve the tortelloni, accompanied by a crisp salad as a main course, or on their own as a starter, in which case this quantity will serve 6.

SERVES 4

FRESH PASTA
200 g (7 oz) '00' pasta flour
pinch of salt
2 eggs
STUFFING
175 g (6 oz) cooked ham,
    preferably smoked
125 g (4 oz) gruyère cheese,
    grated
25 g (1 oz) freshly grated
    Parmesan cheese
30 ml (2 tbsp) chopped fresh
    parsley
1 egg yolk
salt and pepper
SAUCE
900 g (2 lb) ripe tomatoes
1 large onion
2 garlic cloves, crushed
1 fresh oregano sprig
75 g (3 oz) butter
handful of freshly torn basil
    leaves
TO SERVE
torn fennel or flat-leaf parsley
freshly grated Parmesan
    cheese

PREPARATION TIME
40 minutes, plus resting
COOKING TIME
3 minutes, plus
20-30 minutes for sauce
FREEZING
Suitable: Stage 5

630 CALS PER SERVING

1. To make the pasta dough, sift the flour and salt into a mound on a clean work surface and make a well in the centre. Break the eggs into this well.

2. Use a fork to gently beat the eggs and gradually draw in the flour. When the mixture begins to thicken, use your hands to mix to a firm dough. Clean the work surface free of crusty flour and knead the dough for 5 minutes until smooth and velvety. Wrap in cling film and leave to rest for 20 minutes.

3. Meanwhile, prepare the stuffing. Put the ham in a food processor or blender and process until finely minced. Add the remaining ingredients and process briefly until evenly mixed. Set aside.

4. To prepare the sauce, immerse the tomatoes in a bowl of boiling water for 30 seconds, then drain and refresh under cold running water. Peel away the skins. Quarter the tomatoes, discard the seeds, then roughly chop the flesh. Peel and quarter the onion. Put the tomatoes into a saucepan with the onion, garlic, oregano and butter. Bring to the boil, lower the heat and simmer, uncovered, for 20-30 minutes until the sauce is thick and pulpy. Discard the onion and oregano. Season with salt and pepper to taste and stir in the basil.

5. To make the tortelloni: roll out the pasta about a quarter at a time, using a pasta machine if possible. Alternatively roll out on a clean surface as thinly as possible. Cut into 7.5 cm (3 inch) squares. Place a teaspoon of stuffing in the centre of each square. Moisten the edges with a little water and fold each square diagonally in half over the filling to form a triangle. Press the edges to seal and bring the two corners together to shape the tortelloni (see technique). Repeat to use all the filling and dough.

6. Bring a large pan of water to the boil. Add the tortelloni and cook for about 3 minutes until the sealed edges are *al dente*, then drain and transfer to a warmed serving dish. Meanwhile reheat the tomato butter sauce and add to the tortelloni. Toss lightly and serve sprinkled with freshly grated Parmesan and torn parsley or fennel.

TECHNIQUE

To shape each tortelloni, hold the triangle at the longest side, then pull the two corners together, wrapping them round the tip of your forefinger. Pinch the corners together where they join.

BRAGIOLI

Bragioli are Maltese beef olives. There are many versions of this traditional dish, this one being adapted from a dish I have enjoyed many times in a restaurant on the island of Gozo, near Malta. Buy slices of beef prepared as for beef olives, or get your butcher to cut thin slices of rump for you.

SERVES 4

3 eggs

175 g (6 oz) pecorino or emmental cheese, grated

45 ml (3 tbsp) chopped fresh parsley

salt and pepper

4 thin slices beef (for beef olives), each about 175 g (6 oz)

4 slices smoked ham (optional)

1 onion

1-2 garlic cloves

45 ml (3 tbsp) olive oil

100 ml (3½ fl oz) red wine

100 ml (3½ fl oz) beef stock

100 ml (3½ fl oz) passata

15 ml (1 tbsp) chopped fresh thyme

thyme sprigs, to garnish

PREPARATION TIME
20 minutes
COOKING TIME
About 2 hours
FREEZING
Not suitable

595 CALS PER SERVING

1. Bring a small pan of water to the boil. Add the eggs and boil for 6 minutes. Cool under cold running water, then shell and chop. Place in a bowl. Stir in the cheese and parsley and season with pepper to taste.

2. Preheat the oven to 180°C (350°F) Mark 4. Lay the beef slices out flat on a wooden board. Beat with a mallet or rolling pin to flatten if necessary, to give slices about 18 x 25 cm (7 x 10 inches). Lay the smoked ham slices on top, if using.

3. Divide the cheese and egg filling between the beef slices. Fold in the ends and roll each up from the longest side. Secure with wooden cocktail sticks or toothpicks.

4. Peel and slice the onion and garlic. Heat 30 ml (2 tbsp) of the oil in a large frying pan. Add the beef rolls and brown quickly over a high heat on all sides. Transfer to a shallow baking dish – large enough to contain them in one layer.

5. Add the remaining oil to the frying pan. Add the onion and garlic and cook over a medium heat for 3-4 minutes until softened. Add the wine and bring to the boil, stirring well to deglaze the pan. Boil for 1 minute, then stir in the stock and passata. Bring back to the boil and stir in the chopped thyme and seasoning.

6. Spoon the sauce over and around the beef and cover the dish tightly with a lid or with foil. Bake in the oven for about 2 hours until tender, turning the bragioli once or twice during cooking. Remove the lid or foil for the last 20 minutes of the cooking time to allow the sauce to reduce, if preferred. Serve the bragioli hot, garnished with thyme. Accompany with potatoes or rice and a green vegetable.

TECHNIQUE

Fold in the ends of each beef slice, then roll up to enclose the filling. Secure with wooden cocktail sticks or toothpicks.

SPICY SAUSAGES WITH WHITE BEANS AND RED ONION MARMALADE

Throughout the Mediterranean spicy well flavoured sausages are popular, including the Spanish chorizo, French Toulouse and salsiccie of Italy. In this tasty stew, spicy sausages are combined with white beans and served with a sweet 'marmalade' made from red onions. The 'marmalade' can be prepared in advance.

SERVES 4

350 g (12 oz) cannellini
   beans, soaked overnight
2 shallots
2 celery stalks
30 ml (2 tbsp) olive oil
1 garlic clove, crushed
125 g (4 oz) piece streaky
   bacon, diced
15 ml (1 tbsp) each chopped
   fresh thyme and parsley
150 ml ($\frac{1}{4}$ pint) dry white
   wine
2 tomatoes
300 ml ($\frac{1}{2}$ pint) well-flavoured
   stock
salt and pepper
4-8 spicy sausages,
   depending on size
10 ml (2 tsp) olive oil
   (optional)

ONION MARMALADE
4 red onions
30 ml (2 tsp) olive oil
10 ml (2 tsp) chopped fresh
   thyme
120 ml (4 fl oz) red wine
   vinegar
65 g (2$\frac{1}{2}$ oz) caster sugar

TO SERVE
torn flat-leaf parsley

PREPARATION TIME 20 minutes, plus
overnight soaking
COOKING TIME About 1 hour
FREEZING Suitable: Stage 4

645 CALS PER SERVING

1. First prepare the onion marmalade. Halve the red onions and slice them thinly. Heat the oil in a large frying pan. Add the onions and cook over a moderate heat, stirring frequently, for 15-20 minutes until soft and caramelised. Add the thyme, wine vinegar and sugar. Stir until the sugar is dissolved, then increase the heat and let the mixture boil for 4-5 minutes until it is dark and syrupy. Season, then transfer to a bowl to cool.

2. Drain the cannellini beans and place them in a saucepan. Add plenty of fresh cold water to cover. Bring to the boil and boil steadily for 15 minutes. Drain in a colander and set aside.

3. Peel and finely chop the shallots. Finely chop the celery. Heat the oil in a saucepan and add the shallots and celery. Cook over a medium heat, stirring frequently, for 10 minutes until softened and beginning to brown. Stir in the garlic, bacon and herbs and cook for a further 1 minute.

Increase the heat, pour in the white wine and allow to bubble for 2 minutes.

4. Meanwhile, skin, deseed and chop the tomatoes. Add the beans to the pan with the stock and tomatoes. Simmer, covered, for 30-40 minutes or until the beans are tender.

5. Just before serving grill the sausages, or fry them in the oil, if preferred. Serve, sprinkled with parsley, and accompanied by the red onion marmalade.

NOTE: Once cooked you can lay the sausages on top of the beans as they finish cooking to keep warm.

TECHNIQUE

Return the beans to the pan, then add the stock and chopped tomatoes.

PORK AND VEAL KEBABS WITH POLENTA

Meaty kebabs of pork and veal with smoked bacon and sage are served with grilled polenta squares and a simple yogurt and herb sauce. A salad of ripe flavourful tomatoes would make a good accompaniment to this dish.

SERVES 4

POLENTA
200 g (7 oz) polenta (maize meal)
salt
40 g (1 ½ oz) butter
SAUCE
300 ml (½ pint) natural yogurt
1 garlic clove, crushed
45 ml (3 tbsp) chopped mixed fresh herbs, such as parsley and coriander or mint
KEBABS
350 g (12 oz) lean pork
350 g (12 oz) lean veal
125 g (4 oz) streaky bacon
16 sage leaves
60 ml (4 tbsp) olive oil
5 ml (1 tsp) dried oregano
salt and pepper

PREPARATION TIME
45 minutes
COOKING TIME
About 25 minutes
FREEZING
Not suitable

785 CALS PER SERVING

1. First prepare the polenta. Bring 750 ml (1¼ pints) water to the boil in a medium saucepan with a good pinch of salt added. Sprinkle in the polenta, whisking constantly. Bring to the boil, then lower the heat and cook gently for 30-35 minutes, stirring frequently, to give a smooth, thick paste. Stir in the butter and adjust the seasoning.

2. Meanwhile, make the sauce. Stir all the ingredients together in a small bowl. Season with salt and pepper to taste and set aside.

3. Cut the pork and veal into 2 cm (¾ inch) cubes. Cut the streaky bacon into similar sized squares. Thread the pork, veal and bacon onto 4 long kebab skewers, alternating them and tucking in the sage leaves at intervals.

4. Preheat the grill to high. Spread the polenta on a baking tray lined with oiled foil to a 5 mm (¼ inch) thickness. Grill for 3 minutes each side or until golden.

5. Lower the grill setting to medium. Place the kebabs on the grill rack and brush with olive oil. Sprinkle with the oregano, and salt and pepper to taste. Grill for about 15-20 minutes, turning frequently, until browned on all sides and cooked through.

6. To serve, cut the polenta into squares. Arrange on a warmed serving platter with the kebabs. Serve at once, with the yogurt and herb sauce.

NOTE: To save time, use instant polenta which is pre-cooked, following the cooking instructions on the packet.

TECHNIQUE

Thread the pork, veal and bacon cubes onto 4 long kebab skewers, alternating the different meats and interspersing them with the sage leaves at intervals.

PASTA WITH COURGETTES IN A CREAMY TOMATO SAUCE

For this simple, delicately flavoured pasta dish it is essential that the vegetables are correctly cooked. They must be sautéed gently until rich and buttery with a hint of colour. Vary the herbs as you like; tarragon would be a good one to include in place of the dill.

SERVES 4-6

450 g (1 lb) courgettes

1 small onion

2 garlic cloves

4 tomatoes

40 g (1½ oz) butter

400 g (14 oz) dried penne or other pasta

salt and pepper

45 ml (3 tbsp) chopped fresh parsley

30 ml (2 tbsp) chopped fresh dill

300 ml (½ pint) extra-thick double cream

90 ml (6 tbsp) freshly grated Parmesan or pecorino cheese

PREPARATION TIME
20 minutes
COOKING TIME
About 15 minutes
FREEZING
Not suitable

895-595 CALS PER SERVING

1. Trim the courgettes and cut into small dice. Peel and finely chop the onion and garlic.

2. Immerse the tomatoes in a bowl of boiling water for 30 seconds, then drain and refresh under cold running water. Peel away the skins. Quarter the tomatoes, discard the seeds, then chop the flesh.

3. Heat the butter in a large sauté pan. Add the onion and garlic and cook over a gentle heat for 3 minutes until softened.

4. Add the courgettes and increase the heat. Cook, stirring, for about 4 minutes until just beginning to brown, then lower the heat. Cover and cook for a further 3-4 minutes until the courgettes are very tender.

5. Meanwhile, cook the pasta in a large pan of boiling salted water until *al dente* or according to packet instructions.

6. Add the chopped tomatoes and parsley to the courgette mixture and season with salt and pepper to taste. Lower the heat, cover and cook gently for 2 minutes, then stir in the chopped dill and cream. Allow to bubble for 1 minute, then stir in two thirds of the cheese. Cook for a further 1 minute or so, until thickened.

7. Drain the cooked pasta thoroughly, then add to the sauce. Toss to mix. Transfer to a warmed serving bowl or individual plates. Serve at once, sprinkled with the remaining cheese.

VARIATIONS

Flavour the sauce with different herbs, such as parsley and tarragon, or chervil and dill.

TECHNIQUE

Drain the pasta thoroughly in a colander before adding to the sauce.

MUSHROOM AND AUBERGINE RISOTTO

The perfect risotto will be full-flavoured and have a wonderfully creamy texture – the rice absorbing plenty of liquid during cooking whilst retaining its shape well. For best results, use arborio rice – the classic Italian risotto rice with excellent absorption capacity.

SERVES 4

25 g (1 oz) dried porcini
   mushrooms (ceps)
1 aubergine
salt and pepper
175 g (6 oz) fresh
   mushrooms, preferably
   wild
1 small onion
125 g (4 oz) butter
350 g (12 oz) Italian arborio
   rice (see note)
150 ml (¼ pint) dry white
   wine
1.2 litres (2 pints) hot
   chicken or vegetable
   stock
30 ml (2 tbsp) chopped fresh
   parsley
15 ml (1 tbsp) chopped fresh
   sage (optional)
60 ml (4 tbsp) freshly grated
   Parmesan cheese

PREPARATION TIME
20 minutes, plus marinating
COOKING TIME
25-30 minutes
FREEZING
Not suitable

680 CALS PER SERVING

1. Put the dried mushrooms in a small bowl and add warm water to cover. Leave to soak for 20 minutes, then drain, reserving the liquid. Rinse the soaked mushrooms thoroughly, drain, then chop.

2. Trim and dice the aubergine and put into a colander. Sprinkle liberally with salt and leave to degorge for 30 minutes, standing the colander over a plate to catch the bitter juices. Rinse the aubergine thoroughly and drain well.

3. Halve or quarter fresh mushrooms, or leave whole, according to size.

4. Peel and finely chop the onion. Melt half of the butter in a heavy-based saucepan over a medium heat. Add the onion and cook for 5 minutes until softened. Stir in the rice and cook for 2-3 minutes until it is translucent. Add the aubergine and fresh mushrooms. Cook, stirring, for 2 minutes.

5. Add the wine, the chopped porcini and the reserved soaking liquor. Cook for about 3 minutes, until all the liquid is absorbed.

6. Add 600 ml (1 pint) of the stock to the pan, lower the heat, cover and simmer for 10 minutes until the stock is absorbed. Add a further 150 ml (¼ pint)

and continue cooking as before until the liquid is absorbed. Continue to add the stock a ladleful at a time until the rice is tender. This will take 20-25 minutes; it may not be necessary to add all of the stock.

7. Stir in the chopped herbs and remaining butter, together with half of the grated Parmesan. Serve sprinkled with the remaining Parmesan.

NOTE: Arborio rice has the capacity to absorb plenty of liquid during cooking, without turning mushy. It is available from larger supermarkets and delicatessens. You can use long-grain rice as an alternative if necessary, but you will need to use less stock.

TECHNIQUE

Put the diced aubergine in a colander over a plate and sprinkle with salt. Leave to stand for 30 minutes to degorge the bitter juices.

VEGETABLE COUSCOUS WITH HARISSA

Couscous is a staple food in Algeria, Morocco and Tunisia, and is produced from semolina grains. It is often served with chicken or lamb or – as it is here – with a tasty vegetable stew. Harissa, the traditional accompaniment, is a fiery hot red chilli paste, flavoured with garlic, coriander, cumin and mint. It is used widely in North African cookery and is available from ethnic shops in tubes or small cans. If you can't find it, make your own substitute (see below).

SERVES 4-6

2 small onions

1 bunch of baby fennel, or
   1 large fennel bulb

225 g (8 oz) pumpkin

225 g (8 oz) small whole
   baby carrots

450 g (1 lb) quick-cook
   couscous

40 g (1½ oz) butter

2 garlic cloves, crushed

good pinch of saffron
   strands

2 cinnamon sticks

30 ml (2 tbsp) coriander
   seeds, crushed

5 ml (1 tsp) paprika

1 red chilli

225 g (8 oz) tomatoes

225 g (8 oz) courgettes

175 g (6 oz) shelled fresh or
   frozen broad beans
   (optional)

50 g (2 oz) raisins

450 ml (¾ pint) vegetable
   stock

salt and pepper

15 ml (1 tbsp) harissa paste
   (see right)

chopped coriander, to
   garnish

PREPARATION TIME 30 minutes
COOKING TIME About 20 minutes
FREEZING Not suitable

445-300 CALS PER SERVING

1. Peel and quarter the onions, Trim baby fennel; quarter, core and chop large fennel, if using. Peel and chop the pumpkin. Trim and scrub the carrots.

2. Put the couscous in a bowl and moisten with some water, according to the packet instructions. Drain well and place in a steamer or colander lined with muslin. Steam over boiling water for about 20 minutes, forking it through occasionally, until tender and fluffed up.

3. Meanwhile, cook the vegetables. Melt the butter in a large saucepan and add the onions, garlic, fennel, pumpkin and carrots. Cook, stirring, for 3 minutes. Crumble in the saffron and stir in the cinnamon, coriander, paprika and chilli. Lower the heat, cover and cook for 5 minutes.

4. In the meantime, finely slice the chilli; skin and chop the tomatoes; thickly slice the courgettes; skin the broad beans if using. Add these vegetables to the saucepan with the raisins and stock. Season with salt and pepper to taste.

Cook, uncovered, over a medium heat for 10-12 minutes, stirring frequently, until the vegetables are tender and the stock has reduced a little.

5. Just before serving, pour about 200 ml (7 fl oz) of the cooking liquor into a small bowl and stir in the harissa paste.

6. Pile the couscous onto a warmed platter or individual plates and top with the vegetables. Sprinkle with coriander and serve with the harissa sauce.

HARISSA PASTE: If unobtainable, flavour 30 ml (2 tbsp) tomato purée with a little crushed garlic and paprika and cayenne to taste. Use as a substitute.

TECHNIQUE

Fork through the couscous occasionally during cooking, to break up any lumps.

SALADE NIÇOISE

The ingredients of this dish – tomatoes, garlic, tuna, anchovies, olives and eggs – epitomise the Provence region of France. In Nice very small black olives are used. These are full-flavoured, yet without bitterness, and are macerated in oil with flavourings to delicious effect.

SERVES 4

2 tuna steaks, each about
　200 g (7 oz)
olive oil, for basting
4 eggs
175 g (6 oz) thin French
　beans
225 g (8 oz) ripe tomatoes
I crisp lettuce heart, or a
　large handful of salad
　leaves
I red or mild onion
½ cucumber
50 g (2 oz) can anchovies,
　drained
handful of black olives
DRESSING
75 ml (5 tbsp) olive oil
15 ml (I tbsp) white wine
　vinegar
I garlic clove, crushed
salt and pepper
TO GARNISH
30 ml (2 tbsp) roughly torn
　flat-leaf parsley

PREPARATION TIME
20 minutes
COOKING TIME
15 minutes
FREEZING
Not suitable

465 CALS PER SERVING

I. Preheat the grill to medium. Put the tuna steaks on the grill rack and brush with olive oil. Grill for about 7 minutes each side, until firm and cooked through, basting frequently with the oil. Allow to cool, then cut the tuna into chunks.

2. Meanwhile, bring a small pan of water to the boil. Add the eggs, bring back to the boil and cook for 5 minutes, then cool under cold running water and remove the shells.

3. Trim the French beans and add to a pan of boiling water. Cook for 2-3 minutes until barely tender. Drain and refresh under cold running water, then dry on kitchen paper.

4. Cut the tomatoes into wedges. Tear the lettuce into bite-sized pieces. Peel and thinly slice the onion and cucumber.

5. Put all the vegetables in a large salad bowl and toss lightly to mix. Quarter the eggs and add to the salad with the tuna, anchovies and olives. Toss lightly.

6. To make the dressing, whisk all the ingredients together in a small bowl or shake together in a screw-topped jar. Pour over the salad and sprinkle with the parsley. Serve at once.

VARIATION

In place of the fresh tuna, use one 200 g (7 oz) can tuna in oil, drained and flaked.

TECHNIQUE

Slice the grilled tuna into chunks.

GRILLED STUFFED PEPPER SALAD

A colourful salad full of flavours evocative of the Mediterranean – smoky grilled peppers, aromatic fennel and garlic, and a sweet balsamic vinegar dressing. Serve it accompanied by some firm, country bread to mop up all the delicious juices.

SERVES 6

3 small onions
3 red peppers
3 yellow peppers
3 garlic cloves, peeled
45 ml (3 tbsp) capers
25 ml (1½ tbsp) fennel seeds
90 ml (6 tbsp) olive oil
30 ml (2 tbsp) balsamic
  vinegar
45 ml (3 tbsp) roughly torn
  fresh flat-leaf parsley
coarse sea salt and pepper

PREPARATION TIME
About 20 minutes
COOKING TIME
About 20 minutes
FREEZING
Not suitable

200 CALS PER SERVING

1. Peel the onions, leaving the root end intact, and cut into quarters. Drop them into a pan of boiling water and cook for 1 minute; drain well.

2. Preheat the grill to high. Halve the peppers lengthwise cutting through the stems, then core and deseed them. Arrange on the grill rack, skin-side up, in a single layer (see note). Place the onion quarters and garlic cloves on the rack too. Grill until the pepper skins are blistered and well charred. Turn the onions and garlic as necessary, but let them char slightly too.

3. Place the peppers in a bowl, cover with a plate and allow to cool slightly, then peel away their skins. Arrange the peppers on a serving platter. Fill the cavities with the grilled onions and capers.

4. Put the fennel seeds in a dry frying pan and toast over a moderate heat for a few minutes until they begin to pop and release their aroma. Transfer to a mortar and pestle and coarsely grind them. Add the grilled garlic and grind to a paste. Transfer the garlic paste to a small bowl and whisk in the oil and vinegar.

5. Sprinkle the parsley, sea salt and pepper over the salad and spoon on the dressing. Serve at room temperature.

NOTE: If you have a small grill, it may be necessary to grill the peppers in two batches.

TECHNIQUE

Grill the peppers, onion quarters and garlic cloves until charred, turning the onions and garlic from time to time.

TOMATO AND ROASTED BREAD SALAD

This colourful, gutsy salad is full of interesting flavours and textures. To enjoy it at its best serve it outdoors, in the sunshine with a glass of white wine or two.

SERVES 4

2 red or green peppers

1 red onion

1/2 cucumber

1 small fennel bulb

6 ripe plum tomatoes

handful of stoned black olives, halved

handful of fresh basil leaves, shredded

15 ml (1 tbsp) chopped fresh oregano

salt and pepper

225 g (8 oz) firm-textured country bread, crusts removed

25 g (1 oz) butter, melted

DRESSING

75 ml (5 tbsp) olive oil

30 ml (2 tbsp) balsamic vinegar

1/2-1 garlic clove, crushed

PREPARATION TIME
20 minutes
COOKING TIME
About 25 minutes
FREEZING
Not suitable

530 CALS PER SERVING

1. Preheat the grill to high. Halve and deseed the peppers and arrange, skin-side up, on the grill rack. Cook under the grill until the skin is blistered and blackened all over. Allow to cool slightly, then remove the papery skins. Cut the pepper flesh into thin strips and set aside.

2. Preheat the oven to 200°C (400°F) Mark 6. Peel and thinly slice the onion. Peel and dice the cucumber. Quarter, core and chop the fennel. Cut the tomatoes into wedges. Place these ingredients in a bowl with the reserved pepper strips, olives and herbs. Season with salt and pepper to taste and toss lightly.

3. Brush the bread slices with melted butter on all sides, then cut 2.5 cm (1 inch) cubes. Brush a shallow baking tin with butter. Arrange the bread cubes in the tin in a single layer. Bake in the oven for 8-12 minutes until crisp and golden brown.

4. Meanwhile, make the dressing. In a small bowl, mix together the olive oil, balsamic vinegar and garlic. Drizzle over the salad, add the piping hot croûtons and toss again. Serve at once.

TECHNIQUE

When the grilled peppers are cool enough to handle, peel away the papery skins.

ROASTED ASPARAGUS SALAD

Roasting is a great way to cook asparagus. There is no water added so the true flavour of the vegetable is not 'diluted'. The cooking time applies to stalks of medium thickness and should be increased if you are using fatter asparagus stems.

SERVES 4-6

700 g (1 ½ lb) asparagus
   spears
90 ml (6 tbsp) olive oil
45 ml (3 tbsp) lemon juice
coarse sea salt and pepper
TO SERVE
rocket leaves
lemon wedges
Parmesan cheese shavings
   (optional)

PREPARATION TIME
10 minutes
COOKING TIME
About 20 minutes
FREEZING
Not suitable

275-180 CALS PER SERVING

1. Preheat the oven to 200°C (400°F) Mark 6. Trim the asparagus spears and use a potato peeler to peel the bottom 5 cm (2 inches) of each stalk. Arrange the asparagus in a shallow roasting tin.

2. Spoon 60 ml (4 tbsp) of the olive oil over the asparagus and shake lightly to mix. Roast in the oven for about 20 minutes until just tender, turning the asparagus spears once during cooking. Allow to cool.

3. To serve, spoon the remaining olive oil over the asparagus and sprinkle with the lemon juice. Season with coarse sea salt and freshly ground black pepper and toss lightly. Serve with rocket leaves and lemon wedges. Sprinkle with finely pared shavings of Parmesan, if liked.

TECHNIQUE

Peel the base of each asparagus stalk, using a swivel potato peeler.

MELON GRANITA

This Sicilian water ice with its grainy, slushy texture and sweet scent of ripe melons is a most refreshing dessert. It is the ideal choice when summer temperatures are soaring. Crisp, thin biscuits, flavoured with vanilla and orange, are the perfect complement.

SERVES 4-6

GRANITA
125 g (4 oz) sugar
120 ml (4 fl oz) water
2 small ripe melons, such as
    Charentais, Galia or
    Canteloupe
juice of 1 small orange

BISCUITS
225 g (8 oz) butter, at room
    temperature
225 g (8 oz) caster sugar
300 g (10 oz) plain flour
5 ml (1 tsp) baking powder
1 egg
15 ml (1 tbsp) double cream
2.5 ml-5 ml ($\frac{1}{2}$-1 tsp)
    natural vanilla extract
finely grated rind of 1 small
    orange
icing sugar, for dusting

PREPARATION TIME
15 minutes, plus freezing;
15 minutes for biscuits
COOKING TIME
10 minutes
FREEZING
Suitable, including biscuits

215-145 CALS PER SERVING

1. To make the biscuit dough, put all the ingredients except the icing sugar in a large bowl. Mix together until evenly blended to give a smooth dough. Form into a roll, about 5 cm (2 inches) in diameter, and wrap in cling film or non-stick baking parchment. Chill for about 1 hour until firm enough to slice.

2. For the granita, set the freezer to fast-freeze. Put the sugar and water in a small saucepan and heat gently, stirring, until the sugar has dissolved. Bring to the boil and boil, without stirring, for 3 minutes. Remove from the heat and leave to cool completely.

3. Cut the melons in half. Discard the seeds and scoop out the flesh. Place the flesh in a blender or food processor with the orange juice and process until smooth. Transfer to a bowl.

4. Stir about two thirds of the cooled sugar syrup into the melon purée. Test for sweetness before adding the remainder to taste (see note).

5. Turn into a freezerproof container and freeze until the mixture is slushy and beginning to set around the sides, then break up the granules of ice and stir them towards the centre. Repeat this procedure at 30 minute intervals to ensure an even-textured result until the melon mixture is completely frozen into ice crystals.

6. Meanwhile, bake the biscuits. Preheat the oven to 190°C (375°F) Mark 5. Line 2 large baking sheets with non-stick baking parchment. Cut the chilled dough into very thin slices and place, well apart, on the prepared baking sheets. Bake for about 10 minutes until firm and just lightly browned around the edges. Cool slightly, then lift on to a wire rack to cool completely. If desired, lay the biscuits on a rolling pin to curl as they cool for a pretty effect. Dust lightly with icing sugar before serving.

7. To serve, stir the granita and spoon into stemmed glasses. Accompany with the vanilla and orange biscuits.

NOTE: Freezing will lessen the sweetness to a degree, so flavour the purée accordingly.

The calorie count applies to the granita only; each biscuit contains 80 cals.

TECHNIQUE

Break up and stir the ice crystals at 30 minute intervals during freezing.

HONEY ICE CREAM WITH STUFFED DATES

This rich creamy ice with its distinctive honey flavour is accompanied by fresh dates which are stuffed with a delectable lemon-scented pistachio filling. Choose a 'mono-floral' honey such as orange blossom or lavender, if you can, to give a subtly perfumed sweetness to the ice cream.

SERVES 6

ICE CREAM
600 ml (1 pint) whipping cream
200 g (7 oz) clear scented honey, preferably orange blossom

STUFFED DATES
12 fresh dates
50 g (2 oz) shelled pistachio nuts (unsalted)
juice of ½ small lemon
25 g (1 oz) demerera sugar

TO DECORATE
finely pared lemon rind shreds (optional)

PREPARATION TIME
20 minutes
COOKING TIME
Nil
FREEZING
Not suitable

600 CALS PER SERVING

1. Set the freezer to fast-freeze.

2. To make the ice cream, put the cream in a large bowl and whip until it forms soft peaks. Fold in the honey. Transfer the mixture to a freezerproof container, cover and freeze for about 1 ½ hours or until slushy.

3. Remove the ice cream from the freezer and whisk until smooth. Re-cover and return to the freezer until solid.

4. When the ice cream is ready to serve, prepare the stuffed dates. Place the pistachio nuts in a food processor or blender and process briefly to chop finely. Add the lemon rind and juice, and the demerara sugar. Process for a few seconds until the mixture forms a stiff paste.

5. Slit open the dates lengthwise and remove their stones. Stuff the dates with the pistachio paste, dividing it equally between them.

6. Scoop the ice cream into glass serving dishes and sprinkle with lemon rind shreds to decorate if desired. Serve accompanied by the stuffed dates.

VARIATION

Drain 6 pieces of preserved stem ginger in syrup. Finely dice and fold into the cream with the honey.

TECHNIQUE

Spoon the pistachio paste into the stoned dates, dividing it equally between them.

TIRAMISU

Tiramisu literally means 'whip me up' and this explains how easy it is to prepare this popular velvety smooth Italian dessert. It is the rich mascarpone and coffee liqueur which makes it a totally indulgent experience. If preferred, you can use savoiadi (sponge fingers) instead of cake.

SERVES 6-8

250 ml (8 fl oz) hot strong coffee
10 ml (2 tsp) brown sugar
125 ml (4 fl oz) coffee liqueur, such as **Tia Maria** or **Kahlua**
3 eggs, separated
75 g (3 oz) caster sugar
350 g (12 oz) mascarpone cheese
125 ml (4 fl oz) Marsala
225 g (8 oz) Madeira cake or plain sponge
50-75 g (2-3 oz) plain chocolate, grated
TO FINISH
30 ml (2 tbsp) cocoa powder
chocolate curls (optional)

PREPARATION TIME
25 minutes, plus chilling
COOKING TIME
Nil
FREEZING
Not suitable

670-500 CALS PER SERVING

1. Sweeten the coffee with the brown sugar and allow to cool, then stir in the coffee liqueur.

2. Put the egg yolks and sugar in a large bowl and beat until the mixture is pale and thick, then gradually beat in the mascarpone. Stir in the Marsala.

3. In a separate bowl, whisk the egg whites until they stand in stiff peaks. Carefully fold into the mascarpone mixture.

4. Cut the sponge cake into 2 cm (¾ inch) thick slices. Arrange in a layer over the base of a 1.2 litre (2 pint) glass serving bowl. Pour the cooled coffee mixture evenly over the cake and leave for a few minutes until absorbed.

5. Spoon two thirds of the cheese mixture over the sponge and scatter with half of the grated chocolate. Cover with the rest of the cheese mixture and top with the remaining chocolate. Chill in the refrigerator for at least 1 hour.

6. To serve, dust with a little sifted cocoa and decorate with chocolate curls if desired.

CHOCOLATE CURLS: Spread melted plain chocolate on a marble slab to a depth of 5 mm (¼ inch). When just set, draw a fine-bladed knife across the surface of the chocolate at a 45° angle to shave off curls.

VARIATION

As an alternative to mascarpone, you could use a blend of cream cheese and thick cream. Although not quite so rich the result is still pretty good.

TECHNIQUE

Carefully fold the whisked egg whites into the mascarpone mixture until evenly blended.

Fresh fig tart

Plump, soft ripe figs, bathed in a red wine glaze, sit proud on a rich franzipan base which is flavoured with cinnamon and brandy or rum. Serve this heavenly tart with dollops of thick yogurt or crème fraîche, a scoop of vanilla ice or a drizzle of cream.

SERVES 6-8

PASTRY
175 g (6 oz) plain flour
75 g (3 oz) chilled butter, in pieces
40 g (1½ oz) caster sugar
2 egg yolks
a little cold water, to mix

FILLING
100 g (3½ oz) ground almonds
75 g (3 oz) soft light brown sugar
5 ml (1 tsp) ground cinnamon
1 egg, beaten
100 ml (3½ fl oz) dark rum or brandy
6-8 fresh figs, depending on size

GLAZE
175 ml (6 fl oz) red wine
2.5 ml (½ tsp) finely grated lemon rind
75 g (3 oz) caster sugar

PREPARATION TIME
40 minutes, plus chilling
COOKING TIME
30-35 minutes
FREEZING
Not suitable

540-410 CALS PER SERVING

1. To make the pastry, sift the flour into a large bowl. Using your fingertips, lightly rub in the butter, then stir in the sugar. Add the egg yolks and mix to a firm dough using a round-bladed knife, adding a little cold water if necessary. Knead lightly, then wrap in cling film and chill in the refrigerator for 20 minutes.

2. Preheat the oven to 220°C (425°F) Mark 7. Roll out the pastry thinly on a lightly floured surface and use to line a 25 cm (10 inch) fluted flan tin. Chill for a further 20 minutes.

3. Line the pastry case with crumpled foil and bake 'blind' in the oven for 10 minutes. Remove the foil and bake for a further 5 minutes to cook the base.

4. Meanwhile, prepare the filling. In a bowl, mix together the ground almonds, brown sugar and cinnamon. Stir in the beaten egg and rum or brandy to give a soft paste.

5. Spread the almond paste in the base of the pastry case. Bake in the oven for 15-20 minutes until golden and just firm.

6. Meanwhile prepare the glaze. Put the red wine, lemon rind and sugar into a saucepan and dissolve over a low heat. Bring to the boil and simmer until reduced to a light syrup.

7. Peel the figs if necessary (see note) and cut lengthwise into quarters. Arrange on top of the tart. Brush the figs and the surface of the tart with the glaze. Serve the tart warm or cold, but not chilled.

NOTE: Depending on the figs you buy, it may not be necessary to peel them. Judge for yourself – if the skins are thin leave them on.

TECHNIQUE

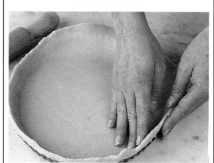

Line the flan tin with the pastry, carefully pressing it into the edges and flutes. Trim off excess pastry.

CLAFOUTIS

Sweet cherries are baked in a custard-like batter and served warm with a dusting of vanilla sugar in this classic French dessert. When fresh cherries are not available, use canned pitted cherries instead.

SERVES 6

700 g (1½ lb) ripe cherries
65 g (2½ oz) butter
4 eggs, plus 2 egg yolks
125 g (4 oz) caster sugar
75 g (3 oz) plain flour
600 ml (1 pint) milk
vanilla sugar, for dusting

PREPARATION TIME
20-30 minutes
COOKING TIME
45-50 minutes
FREEZING
Not suitable

410 CALS PER SERVING

1. Preheat the oven to 190°C (375°F) Mark 5. Wash the cherries and remove their stems and stones. Use 15 g (½ oz) of the butter to grease a shallow round ovenproof dish large enough to hold the cherries. Put the cherries in it.

2. Melt the remaining butter and allow to cool. In a large bowl, beat the eggs and yolks together. Add the sugar and whisk until the mixture is pale and light. Whisk in the cooled melted butter. Gradually sift in the flour, beating well so the mixture is smooth and free of lumps, then mix in the milk.

3. Pour the batter over the cherries and bake in the oven for 45-50 minutes, until the clafoutis is golden and lightly set. Allow to cool slightly. Serve warm, dusted with vanilla sugar.

VARIATION

When fresh cherries are unavailable, use two 425 g (15 oz) cans pitted cherries instead. Drain them thoroughly.

TECHNIQUE

Remove the stones from the cherries, using a cherry stoner if possible. A double-pronged stoner works particularly well.

ITALIAN MERINGUES WITH FRESH FRUITS AND VANILLA SUGAR

Meringues which are crisp and white on the outside but give way to a soft sugary centre make a delightful dessert, especially when they are served with fresh flavourful fruits, cream or yogurt and a sprinkling of vanilla-flavoured sugar.

SERVES 6

MERINGUES
175 g (6 oz) caster sugar
3 egg whites
TO SERVE
**fruits in season, such as
    peaches or nectarines,
    strawberries and
    raspberries**
vanilla sugar
**whipped cream, crème
    fraîche or thick yogurt**

PREPARATION TIME
20 minutes, plus cooling
COOKING TIME
1½-2 hours
FREEZING
Suitable: Meringues only

200 CALS PER SERVING

1. Preheat the oven to its lowest setting, maximum 120°C (250°F) Mark ½. Line two baking sheets with non-stick baking parchment.

2. Put the caster sugar and egg whites in a large heatproof bowl and set this over a pan of gently simmering water. Using an electric whisk, beat on high speed until the mixture is very thick and leaves a very thick 'trail' across the surface when the beaters are lifted. Immediately remove the bowl from the heat and continue whisking for 2 minutes.

3. Using two large spoons, shape the meringue mixture into 12 oval rounds, spacing them apart on the prepared baking sheets. Bake in the oven for 1½-2 hours until the meringues are crisp and can be easily peeled away from the baking parchment (see note). Set aside until cooled.

4. To serve, prepare the fruits as necessary, slicing the peaches or nectarines. Pile the meringues onto a serving plate and arrange the fresh fruits in a separate dish, sprinkling them with the vanilla sugar. Accompany with a bowl of chilled cream, crème fraîche or yogurt.

Alternatively arrange two meringues on each individual plate with the fruits, a dollop of cream or yogurt and a dusting of vanilla sugar.

NOTE: To ensure even cooking, switch the baking sheets around halfway through baking.

TECHNIQUE

Whisk the meringue in a bowl over gently simmering water until the mixture is very thick and leaves a thick trail when the beaters are lifted.

If you would like further information about the **Good Housekeeping Cookery Club**, please write to:
Penny Smith, Ebury Press, Random House, 20 Vauxhall Bridge Road, London SW1V 2SA.